How Fruits and Vegetables Grow

Apples
Grow on a Tree

by Mari Schuh

Consulting Editor: Gail Saunders-Smith, PhD

Consultant: Sarah Pounders, education specialist
National Gardening Association

CAPSTONE PRESS
a capstone imprint

Pebble Books are published by Capstone Press,
151 Good Counsel Drive, P.O. Box 669, Mankato, Minnesota 56002.
www.capstonepub.com

Books published by Capstone Press are manufactured with paper
containing at least 10 percent post-consumer waste.

Library of Congress Cataloging-in-Publication Data
Schuh, Mari C., 1975–
  Apples grow on a tree / by Mari Schuh.
    p. cm.—(Pebble books. How fruits and vegetables grow)
  Summary: "Simple text and photographs describe how apples grow on trees"—
Provided by publisher.
  Includes bibliographical references and index.
  ISBN 978-1-4296-5279-7 (library binding)
  ISBN 978-1-4296-6181-2 (paperback)
  1. Apples—Juvenile literature. I. Title. II. Series: Pebble (Mankato, Minn.). How
fruits and vegetables grow.
  SB363.S38 2011
  634'.11—dc22   2010025469

Note to Parents and Teachers

The How Fruits and Vegetables Grow set supports national science
standards related to life science. This book describes and illustrates
how apples grow on trees. The images support early readers in
understanding the text. The repetition of words and phrases helps
early readers learn new words. This book also introduces early
readers to subject-specific vocabulary words, which are defined in
the Glossary section. Early readers may need assistance to read some
words and to use the Table of Contents, Glossary, Read More, Internet
Sites, and Index sections of the book.

Printed in the United States of America in North Mankato, Minnesota.
092010
005933CGS11

Table of Contents

4

From Tree to Table

Rows and rows of trees fill orchards. The trees grow fruits and nuts for people to eat.

Life Cycle of an Apple Tree

seeds

seedling

flowers

apples

6

Trees make fruits
and nuts in similar ways.
Apples are one fruit
that grows on trees.

seeds

fruit

branch

leaves

trunk

Seeds and Buds

Apple trees start as tiny brown seeds. The seeds slowly grow into trees. After four to eight years, the tree is ready to grow apples.

9

Spring is here. Buds grow on the branches. The buds open into pink and white flowers. Each flower has pollen inside.

Pollination

Bees spread pollen.
Pollen fertilizes the flower
to make a seed.
Apples begin to grow.
They will hold the seeds.

Growing and Ripening

In summer, tree leaves turn sunlight and gases into sugars. These sugars help apples grow big and juicy. In fall, most apples are ripe.

16

In winter, the tree
is dormant. It rests
to save its energy
for spring.

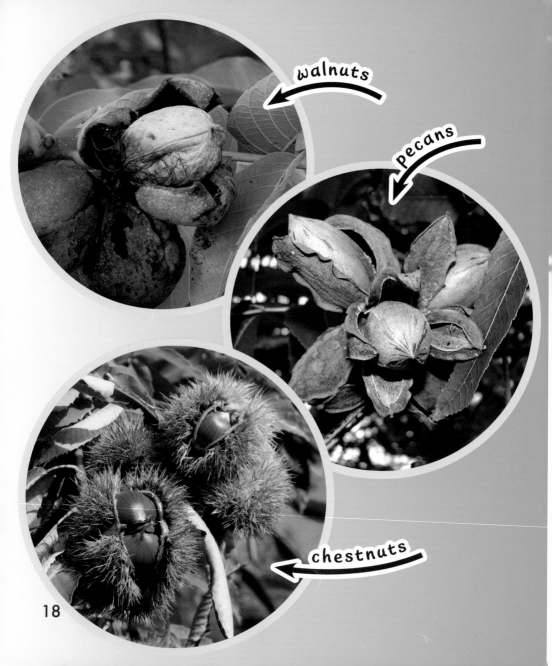

walnuts

pecans

chestnuts

18

Trees Grow Many Foods

Many foods begin their lives on trees. Walnuts, pecans, and chestnuts grow on trees.

olives

peaches

avocados

Fruits such as olives, peaches, and avocados come from trees. Each year, trees give us healthy food to eat.

Glossary

avocado—a green or black pear-shaped fruit with a tough skin and creamy, light green pulp inside

bud—a small shoot on a plant that grows into a leaf or a flower

dormant—a state of rest

fertilize—when pollen from the male part of the flower joins with the ovum from the female part of the flower to produce a seed

fruit—the part of a plant that contains seeds

olive—a small black or green fruit that is eaten whole or crushed for its oil

orchard—a field or farm where fruit and nut trees grow

pollen—tiny yellow grains in flowers

pollinate—to carry pollen from flower to flower

ripe—ready to be harvested, picked, or eaten

Read More

Royston, Angela. *Life Cycle of an Apple*. Heinemann First Library. Chicago: Heinemann Library, 2009.

Spilsbury, Louise. *Fruits*. Eat Smart. Chicago: Heinemann Library, 2009.

Tagliaferro, Linda. *The Life Cycle of an Apple Tree*. Plant Life Cycles. Mankato, Minn.: Capstone Press, 2007.

Internet Sites

FactHound offers a safe, fun way to find Internet sites related to this book. All of the sites on FactHound have been researched by our staff.

Here's all you do:

Visit *www.facthound.com*

Type in this code: 9781429652797

Check out projects, games and lots more at
www.capstonekids.com

Index

Word Count: 170
Grade: 1
Early-Intervention Level: 21

Editorial Credits
Erika L. Shores, editor; Bobbie Nuytten, designer; Wanda Winch, media researcher;
    Laura Manthe, production specialist

Photo Credits
Capstone Press: Karon Dubke, 6 (bottom); Dwight R. Kuhn, 6 (top right); iStockphoto:
Zeljana Dubrovic, 18 (top); Shutterstock: Anastasiya Igolkina, 10, Antoinette W, 20
(bottom), Constant, 8, Elena Elisseeva, cover (green background), 4, 14, Gorilla, 12
(top right), Hydromet, 6 (middle), inacio pires, 20 (top), Jiri Vaclavek, 20 (middle),
John A. Anderson, 6 (top left), 8 (top left), LianeM, cover (middle), Patrick Morand,
18 (bottom), Ruslan Kokarev, 12, TFoxFoto, 16, Vaclav Volrab, (apple element used
throughout book), Victoria Field, 18 (middle)

The author dedicates this book to her niece Camryn Schuh of Mankato, Minnesota.